Values to ValYOUable

- A Simple 3-Step Approach to Recognition and Rewards

Dick C. Waters

Values to ValYOUable

(Revised Edition - November 2022)

© 2022 Dick C. Waters

All Rights Reserved. No part of this book may be reproduced in any form or by any means without the prior consent of Dick C. Waters, except brief quotes used in reviews.

WARNING: Making copies or distributing this file, either on disc, paper, CD, or over the Internet is a Federal Offense under the U.S. Copyright Act, and a violation of several International Trade Agreements.

ISBN 9798351930930

Feedback is very much appreciated – Thank you!

Email to dickcwaters@gmail.com

Link to Amazon Author Page -

https://www.amazon.com/Dick-Waters/e/B007K8J222

(Includes Many Book-Trailer Videos)

VALUES TO VALYOUABLE – A 3-STEP APPROACH TO RECOGNITION AND REWARDS

Contents

- Foreword 4
- Track Field Dedication 15
- Dedication 16
- Overview 18
- History 21
- References 23
- Exercise 31
- Indispensable People 32
- Introduction to Values 35
- Impact of Values on Recognition and Rewards ... 37
- Values for Consideration 39
  - On a PERSONAL Level 39
  - On a MANAGERIAL Level 45
  - On a BUSINESS Level 54
  - On a PROJECT Level 61
  - Of a GENERAL Nature 66
- Summary List of My Values 72
- My Credentials 74
- Closing Remarks 76
- Index 78
- Bibliography 81
- Author Books and Amazon Page 82

Foreword

I am hoping to get your attention to this book.

Hear these two words -

"Great Job!"

What an inspiration when you hear those words.

VALUES TO VALYOUABLE – A 3-STEP APPROACH TO RECOGNITION AND REWARDS

Those words can inspire you. You have been recognized for doing something wonderful. But what if you have not heard those words from your boss, or even a teammate? What if you hear them given to someone else? What did that person do to be recognized?

If you are the person getting that recognition, you should write me to let me know what your formula is to being a high performer. You might be interested in what I am suggesting for people to do to be a more valuable performer, and to be properly recognized and rewarded.

Many people over the course of their careers spend years on; education, training, obtaining experience, and developing skills to help them establish themselves and to be rewarded.

Most likely you worked hard to secure your current position. Now that you have that job, how can you be even more successful? The goal of this book is to help YOU define a 'values path' to being a more valuable performer, and an asset to your company.

Why do I believe you can do this? That is a great question. I have not proven it yet, but with your help, I will be able to show how many people have succeeded. I want your feedback after you read this book, and have defined your success model, written it down, and followed it religiously.

Right now, I only have what it did for me. That one-page sheet changed my life, by reinforcing what was important to me, and how I approached work.

I will get into how values ties to principles later, but right now, think of this – do you have a personal mission statement? Let's start with companies. Most, if not all, companies have constructed a company mission statement. They believe that their employees as well as customers need to know what they stand for. Many spend considerable funds along with effort to define their prime values. I believe it is important for everyone working to define their own mission statement.

Looking back at my own working situation, I didn't have one to start and that is an important point. However, I always worked in a certain manner. I knew what work manner made me happy, and I also knew what work manners of others bothered me.

It wasn't until the high-tech Fortune 500 company I was working for at the time, decided to go on a Quality mission. To make a long-story short, I had a discussion with my boss about quality starting at the worker level. It was great that the company was focusing on quality, all companies should do that, but people make quality happen. A company can create a banner, but the employees need to deliver quality results. He smiled at me, and that response upset me enough to take some action.

VALUES TO VALYOUABLE – A 3-STEP APPROACH TO RECOGNITION AND REWARDS

What I did in the next few hours was to understand what I stood for and what was driving me. What I didn't understand at that time was that this effort was going to direct my performance for the rest of my career. I defined my Values Sheet. No longer was it only in my head, but I had something on paper that would consistently lead me down the path of more valuable performance. It wasn't exactly a road map, but it was the rules of my road. It was how I was driving myself.

I'll elaborate on how that single piece of paper opened doors for me, reinforced my attitude and direction, and allowed others to challenge me if I did not live up to those standards.

If this worked for me, I honestly believe it will work for you. I believe this so strongly, that I have committed myself to define this for you. I don't need this, but I believe that it can change many peoples' careers and make them more valuable performers. I purposely kept this book short as I wanted as many people as possible to read it. This simple read and only a few hours of effort, can make a difference in your career. Please trust me, I am helping you get where you want to go. That is one of the values on my values sheet –

Help my people, and others, get where they want to go.

There is also another closely related value to this book effort –

Go after VICTORIES that are worth winning.

Those are just two examples, simply stated, but when followed, can lead a person to be more successful. When you read the following pages, you will learn more about me, what my background was, what I did for a career, and how each of my values helped guide me.

If you owned a company, would you want

A Most Valuable Performer/Player, or would you want <u>many</u> M V P's?

If this book does help you be more successful, please share it with some friends or associates.

Let me continue to hopefully get your attention.

Have you ever noticed someone at school or work who managed to capture everyone's attention? No, I'm not talking about that very attractive person...I'm talking about that person who garners everyone's attention by what they do.

Have you ever been that person? If you have, the feeling is a great one. It has a way of compounding itself. One success facilitates another, and soon people are talking about YOU. Rewards in the form of positive reviews, compensation, opportunities and even promotions happen.

VALUES TO VALYOUABLE – A 3-STEP APPROACH TO RECOGNITION AND REWARDS

The interesting thing is that not all these people have the highest degrees from the best schools, many years of experience, or even significant training. Then, if these are not the things that fuel their success, what is?

I'm not going to answer that right now. I want you to think of someone you noticed, or are noticing currently, and consider their background and what is making you pay attention to them? You might be one of the lucky ones who can consider themselves in this category. What about them makes them standout and be recognized? I suggest you stop reading and make some notes.

Why? My hope is that this book can identify some things that can help you be one of these recognized people. I have some personal characteristics that helped me become highly recognized, but more importantly, I believe that everyone can identify their own individual attributes that fuels, or can fuel, being a valuable asset to a company.

Who am I to suggest this? I'm not a doctor, I'm not currently a lecturer, and I don't have a Master's degree. However, what I do have is enough years of business experience to know the difference between just existing in an organization and being a driving force. Not so much a driving force to others, as one to myself.

What changed my just being a player to being a leader was something I want you to do for yourself. If I can help one person make a difference in their career, this book will have been more than worth the effort.

This book is hard for me to write. I have several self-published novels that I cranked out in a relatively short period of time. They are works of fiction, where I just let my mind take me where it wanted to go. I have a creative mind and after retirement, my wife told me to either go back to work, or find something to do. Writing novels fits that puzzle. However, writing a non-fiction book has been harder.

VALUES TO VALYOUABLE – A 3-STEP APPROACH TO RECOGNITION AND REWARDS

Unlike a novel, there is no beginning, middle and end...there is just a whole pile of things that need to be organized into something I hope will do the trick for anyone who wants to give it a try.

Back to just a player to a leader. I worked for several high-technology firms for over forty years and it is important for me to mention them. One of the common denominators in every one of these firms and individual departments were the managers I had. They deserve most of the credit for most of my successes. They were supportive and let me run with my ideas. Many times, they were diametrically opposed to my thinking. However, I was so committed to my ideas that I was driven to prove them wrong. I'll explain that in more detail shortly.

I started work at eighteen at Sylvania. My first job was working in the mailroom. My parents worked for that company, and my dad believed in me enough to vouch for me to get me that job.

Later, after four years working in their engineering department dealing with proposals, my boss suggested that I entertain a job at an up-and-coming computer company.

She had a friend at that company, and they were looking for people like me. If I was interested, she would contact that person.

I learned a very important management lesson from her, to help other people get where they need to go.

That small company became part of Honeywell.

I got the job and spent sixteen years working my way up the Honeywell information systems arena. My claim to fame is my analytical ability. I was good at drawing pictures of processes and pointing out the shortcomings, but more importantly, how to do the process much more efficiently.

I later followed one boss to Wang Laboratories and spent 9 years there. That is where something happened that changed how I was recognized.

Wang Labs was launching a major initiative on quality and customer satisfaction. I would like to think that this was fate, but maybe it was my destiny. I had a discussion with my boss that I felt that although the company was pushing for quality, I commented that quality needed to start with people being focused on their quality.

When his head spun around twice, I knew he didn't understand what the hell I was talking about. I guess out of frustration or a desire to prove my point, I went away and wrote down what I labeled as "My Compass of Values."

VALUES TO VALYOUABLE – A 3-STEP APPROACH TO RECOGNITION AND REWARDS

It only took me about two hours to compile my thoughts onto that paper, but the power that piece of paper had, changed my career. THAT is why I want the opportunity to share this with you. You invested in this book, and my hope and desire are that it will help you change your attitude and performance to enable you to be one of those highly recognized people.

Well, when I reviewed my "Compass of Values" sheet with my boss, his head only spun around once, but I realized the document was for **me**, not him. The interesting thing is that document changed only slightly since its creation in 1990. The other interesting thing is that I don't need to write this book for me, I need to write this for you.

So, in the memory of Ethel, here's one of my values –

> ➤ *HELP my people, and others, get where they want to go.*

One suggestion a former manager gave me after reading the first draft of this book, 'in part, his personal success was finding the right 'role model' to guide his own behavior.

After his comment, I realized that I had done the same thing, which is also a great suggestion for you.

Since writing my compass of values, I have managed to obtain my certification as a PMI Certified Project Manager from the Project Management Institute, along with obtaining four Director-level positions with a Fortune 500 company, including one as Director of Quality. I went all the way from thinking about quality at the individual level to running a quality department.

It is not important that in my own mind I was on the right track back in 1990, but that what we did with quality as an organization was something we were all proud of. In fact, MicroAge QIS in Tempe Arizona won the Arizona Association of Industries' *Manufacturer of the Year Award* two years in a row, and Industry Week Magazine noted us as one of the twenty-five best companies in the world.

Please do yourself a favor. Please write down what makes YOU TICK. Start right now, and keep making notes as you read this book. I am going to share my values along with some stories with the hope it will enable you to write your own set of values, think "what makes you tick." These are your strengths and the things that are going to get your behavior and results recognized and hopefully rewarded.

Track Field Dedication

THE CITIZENS OF THE TOWN OF WILMINGTON PROUDLY DEDICATE THE HIGH SCHOOL TRACK TO FRANCIS P. KELLEY IN RECOGNITION OF HIS COUNTLESS CONTRIBUTIONS TO THE WILMINGTON COMMUNITY AND HIS MANY YEARS OF DEDICATED SERVICE TO THE STUDENTS AND ATHLETES OF WILMINGTON HIGH SCHOOL.

TOWN MEETING, APRIL 23, 2005
DEDICATED, MAY 18, 2006

Dedication

After writing and publishing eight books, you would think it would be easier to write this one. But it has been a struggle. I have found it hard to get the right start. I know what I want to convey and how it might help many people, but I know if the start isn't correct, it will not have reader acceptance.

However, or obviously, I received the inspiration I so needed.

There is a gentleman known as Mister Kelley. More correctly, there was an important man in my life known as Mr. Kelley. He passed away suddenly, but I had the opportunity to see him just before. I told him he had no idea of the lives he touched in a positive manner. So why, you ask, is that the inspiration I so needed?

I cannot put into words in this space the answer to that question. However, I hope I can convey to you in as few words as possible, what that man did for thousands of students and athletes. Whether teaching or coaching, he always preached to do your best and to try to do better the next time.

I tried my best at work to follow that mantra. I realize now, that Mr. Kelley laid the necessary foundation for my professional success. I have one goal I am still trying my best to achieve – to write a 'best-selling' book.

I have tried my best to write a book that will help some people, but only readers can recognize and reward my performance.

VALUES TO VALYOUABLE – A 3-STEP APPROACH TO RECOGNITION AND REWARDS

Attending Mr. Kelley's wake and funeral has reinforced my effort not to give up and to do my best. I believe things happen the way they are supposed to. Specifically, I returned to where I grew up and had the good fortune to have lunch with Mr. Kelley, and a life-long friend, just four days before he passed away in his sleep. My being there during his last days was meant to be.

I can hear his words, "You can do it, keep at it, and do your best."

Why is he associated with this book? He may have preached doing your best, but more importantly, he set an example of standing for values based on a strong set of principles. He impacted so many lives not just based on his teaching and coaching, but by the example he set. I can only try my best to do my part.

This book is my attempt at doing my best to help you to be your best in your career. I honestly believe that what can help you to be better at what you do is not only your education, experience or your skills, but by how you approach what you do. There are some characteristics that you possess currently, that when identified and documented, can be your mantra for future success. I hope I can inspire you to identify them, and to live by them, and by doing so, return my gratitude to my dear friend. I'm trying to pay it forward.

Thank you, Mr. Kelley. I am trying my best and I am not giving up.

If you haven't realized it by now, I am dedicating this book to Mr. Kelley.

With much love, thank you!

Overview

To know yourself is to prevent others from "**NO**ing you."

Are you Not Getting one or more of these things?

- Hired
- Personal Results
- Working up to your potential
- Respect
- New Assignments
- New Responsibilities
- Leadership Roles
- Promoted
- Enjoyment
- Recognition
- Rewards

I believe you already possess the CURE for getting these things.

Three simple steps to create what will become positive habits, recognition and rewards:

1. **Identify your personal values**
2. **Document them**
3. **Follow them**

Most companies in the hiring process focus on these:

- ✓ Education
- ✓ Training
- ✓ Experience
- ✓ Knowledge
- ✓ Learning
- ✓ Skills

But I believe what they are really seeking is someone with the ability to get the positive results they need.

VALUES TO VALYOUABLE – A 3-STEP APPROACH TO RECOGNITION AND REWARDS

I believe that your ATTITUDE and HOW you approach doing things is just as important to obtain positive results as what you do.

It could be summarized as doing **your personal best** and not giving up.

I believe YOU have nothing new to learn. YOU already possess what it takes. All YOU need to do is to list what makes you tick. Your personal values, when identified, documented, and followed, will get you the results that will get you recognized and rewarded.

Why am I sure? Because it worked for me, and it can work for you.

Things changed significantly for me after I defined my Personal Mission Statement (values).

VALUES SUCCESS PATH

		W					R
		O					E
		R					W
		K	R				A
		P	E				R
			S		R		D
V	**A**	**L**	**U**		**E**		**S**
A	T	A	L		C		
L	T	C	T		O		
U	I	E	S		G		
E	T				N		
S	U				I		
	D				T		
	E				I		
					O		
					N		

1. Identify your **Values**
2. Use them with a positive **attitude**
3. In your **Workplace**
4. To get better or improved **results**
5. Hopefully with management **recognition**
6. And the **rewards** that go along with it

VALUES TO VALYOUABLE – A 3-STEP APPROACH TO RECOGNITION AND REWARDS

History

In the 90's, I was working for Wang Laboratories in Massachusetts. The company was placing an increased focus on quality, and ultimately, customer satisfaction. I had a discussion with my boss that quality should start with the individual, focused on his/her own efforts to deliver the highest-quality results. His head spun around a couple of times and I thought it best to take it as a signal that I was off in left field. However, it provided the emphasis that eventually changed my career.

I went away and thought about what I was really trying to communicate. It didn't take me long to identify the aspects of individual focus that would provide quality results. It was surprising that this one-page list came so quickly. The next day, I showed the list to my boss, and this time, his head only spun around once. He still didn't get it…but I certainly did. For the first time in my life, I realized what was driving me. These were the things I believed in and operated by. From that day on, I put "My Compass of Values" in a protective sleeve and used it constantly.

I have used the list in the interview process to get hired by three companies. I have also used the list when seeking other internal opportunities including promotions. I have shared the list with my different staff and asked if they ever witness me not operating in line with it, to call me on it.

More importantly, I have followed that compass to many personal successes. For example, when others thought I was wasting my time going for special company recognition, my values kept me focused –

> ➢ *Go after **VICTORIES** that are worth winning.*
> ➢ *Believe; **"ANYTHING CAN BE DONE,"** it just has a price tag!*

We won the Arizona Association of Industries' Manufacturer of the Year award. And when they said I was wasting my time competing for it a second year, we won it back-to-back! Then, when I wanted to see if Industry Week Magazine would consider our company one of the twenty-five best manufacturing companies, we indeed succeeded.

Winning these awards wasn't a matter of changing what our company was, it was a matter of putting in the effort to complete the required paperwork in a manner that facilitated a clear understanding of our company performance.

> ➢ *Point the right **DIRECTION** and strive for positive **RESULTS***
> ➢ ***ANTICIPATE** and **PLAN** accordingly.*
> ➢ *Communicate with **"PICTURES"** to facilitate understanding.*

References

Without knowing it at the time, I created a life-changing document in an afternoon. I didn't call it a personal mission statement at the time. I have since learned from reading Stephen Covey's *7 Habits of Highly Effective People*, that MY VALUES sheet is a *Personal Mission Statement*.

Perhaps this is the time to mention further Stephen Covey's book *7 Habits of Highly Effective People*. A great book which has been around for over twenty-five years. I've read the book twice and highly recommend it.

First a story. On one of my interviews, the vice-president asked me specifically, "What makes you tick Dick?" I immediately offered him my compass of values sheet. He read the document, smiled and said he had a couple of other people he would like me to talk to. I later realized that the interview was over at that point. I was already hired.

What I learned later was that he was a Covey person. He recognized that my sheet was directed at the Covey teachings. Here are *Covey's 7 Habits* -

Habit 1 – Be Proactive
Habit 2 – Begin with the End in Mind
Habit 3 – Put First Things First
Habit 4 – Think Win/Win
Habit 5 – Seek First to Understand, then to Be Understood
Habit 6 – Synergize
Habit 7 – Sharpen the Saw

In Covey's book, he talked about writing a *Personal Mission Statement*. After reading his book, I believe some of the people's examples were more goals. Goals are things you target to accomplish; they are meant to get completed.

Behaviors are how you act, and what you do and as such, are done continuously. A habit is formed when you do something over and over until it becomes automatic or second nature...a habit. I believe you can establish Stephen's habits, by defining HOW you approach tasks.

What are the personal values that have made you successful in the past? They need to be identified, documented, and followed. They are what separates you from the crowd, and defines how you drive the bus, rather than just riding along. To help you get these identified do the following –

Draw a circle and put your name in it. Now think about your relationship to everyone you meet. Think of it like an expanded organization chart.

You might have a boss, or a parent. You might have workers working for you. You might have others on your team or in your department. You might be part of a project team, or even have multiple projects. Your boss has a higher-level boss, which we could call management.

Maybe you have customers you deal with directly or indirectly. Maybe you are in civil service and there are members of the public.

Regardless, it is important to define each of those. Why? Because the next step is to define how you relate to each area. The values are different working on a team than what you might do to support the overall company.

VALUES TO VALYOUABLE – A 3-STEP APPROACH TO RECOGNITION AND REWARDS

On my one-page list I wound up with five areas –

Let's take the Personal category. These are the values I defined for my actions in that area:

- ❖ *Treat others as I would **CARE** to be treated.* (Yes, it is the Golden rule)
- ❖ *Always be **HONEST***
- ❖ *Build **CREDIBILITY** each and every day*
- ❖ *Be a **VISIONARY** and provide **CREATIVE SOLUTIONS***
- ❖ ***LEARN** from my mistakes*
- ❖ *Be a **CARING** person*

Now, I shared those with you, but what do you stand for, and what do you want to be known for at a personal level?

If you are having a problem with this, think about what ticks you off when you see others behaving badly. Chances are, your beliefs or values are directly opposite that behavior. I am not going to share another list like this, but will be mentioning my values as it becomes appropriate to share each of them with you.

I have a one-page document that has thirty-three listed values. How many are you going to have? This is not a course or a seminar that you have to apply those teachings, you already possess these characteristics or behaviors. The objective is to write them down, and follow them to be more successful and better recognized.

So, what is the power of that sheet of paper? First, it gave me a license to drive the bus, not just be a rider. If someone didn't like how I was operating, they could challenge me on it. However, in the nineteen years after making this list, nobody ever did. In fact, when provided during the job interview process, it got me three jobs. It was also useful during the internal promotion process.

VALUES TO VALYOUABLE – A 3-STEP APPROACH TO RECOGNITION AND REWARDS

I recall an old television program called *Have Gun, Will Travel*. This sheet of paper was my *Have License, Will Drive*. Honestly, once you have your own document, it will indeed give you the license to perform at a much higher and, hopefully, consistent, and recognized level. Who wouldn't want an employee working to a high-level set of values? It is called being valuable. Rewards come from recognition, recognition comes from performance. You can and will do this, and I can help.

First a story –

During the dedication section of this book, I referred to Mr. Kelley. Along with being a highly regarded and demanding high-school mathematics teacher, he was also the track coach. He cheered every track performer, whether they were the fastest runner or the worst shotput thrower. His belief was for the participant to never give up, and to try to better their own personal performance.

Winning the overall track meet was not his driving motivation. Many times, he had someone on the team who would negatively impact the team's ability to win a competition, but he had the person on the team because that person needed the personal satisfaction and reward. He was truly a caring person.

One of his favorite stories was about a young lady who he tried to recruit for cross country. He was always trying to recruit anyone not already on the various track teams. This young lady said she couldn't run because she was handicapped. Mr. Kelley, himself, had TB and walked with a noticeable limp and carried a stick to steady himself. Anyway, she eventually joined the cross-country team.

He worked with her to increase her abilities and performance. He made a deal with her that if she ran the Junior Varsity course (two miles) in under twenty-four minutes, he would reward her with a T-Shirt.

The day of the competition came and all the runners were past the finish line in under twenty minutes. Twenty-one minutes came and no other runner, twenty-two and twenty-three and still no runner in sight. Finally, this young-woman finished the race with ten seconds short of twenty-four minutes.

It was the first time a runner finished the course with a prosthetic leg.

How can you possibly measure the positive impact that run had on that woman's life? He did give her the T-Shirt that read; "Pain is temporary, Pride lasts a lifetime, Glory is forever…Go for the Glory."

VALUES TO VALYOUABLE – A 3-STEP APPROACH TO RECOGNITION AND REWARDS

During Mr. Kelley's memorial service, the person giving part of the eulogy asked who in the audience would carry his stick? The person said he hoped we all would carry it. In essence, to try to pay it forward in Mr. Kelley's name.

That was the motivation I needed to try to finish this book to help anyone else to be highly successful, recognized and rewarded.

At my age, it is about all I can do, but I am not going to give up.

In our early lives, many of us get programmed not to do, or try, something.

"You're just wasting your time."

"That's not going to work."

"Don't be silly"

"You don't have what it takes."

I will not let those early programs tell me that this book will not help anyone. I can't let it stop me. Two of my values are –

> ❖ ***HELP*** *my people and others get where they want to go.*
> ❖ *Be a good **EDUCATOR**, and share past successes and any failures.*

VALUES TO VALYOUABLE – A 3-STEP APPROACH TO RECOGNITION AND REWARDS

Exercise

I recommend now you stop reading. If you can find somewhere private to go and hopefully be totally alone, don't be afraid to close the door. This is the start of your changing how you operate for the rest of your life. Please give yourself a good start.

Now, close your eyes and think about how you look at yourself, and how you want others to see and recognize you. It might be called Values, Your Personal Mission Statement or Your Compass of Values. Right now, you don't need to identify what it is called, but you are trying to identify what makes you tick.

Think about who you meet or how you relate; within the organization, to your boss, to your team, to your staff, to customers, on projects, etc. As you think about something, write it down on a sticky note. To help in the process, think about one of your successes. What drove you? Were you alone, or did you have support? If you were alone, why? Does something really piss you off? If it does, the opposite might be one of your values. We are not talking about goals; we are talking about how you approach things.

Keep these sticky notes and as you think of additional ones, add them, or clarify the others. When you are done, you should have several listed that you are comfortable with that will drive your efforts in the future.

There is no right answer. This is going to be what you stand for, and what will guide your future performance.

Indispensable People

It is time to think about the people we would consider indispensable. We all know some of these people. We have worked with them. They are critical to the business. Without their expertise and participation, the company would surely fail.

Webster's New World Dictionary defines indispensable as –

"*...adj.* **1.** that cannot be dispensed with or neglected. **2.** absolutely necessary or required

n. an indispensable person or thing – *Syn.* ESSENTIAL."

Webster's American Thesaurus lists the synonyms as follows –

"...essential, crucial, vital, imperative, absolutely necessary, needed, required, requisite, not dispensable, needful, obligatory, mandatory, compulsory; fundamental, basic..."

My takeaways from that are these – businesses will not dispense with (terminate) a person whom they deem as indispensable, or neglect (under pay) him/her. We could discuss whether anyone is indispensable. We have all heard the saying, "Cemeteries are filled with indispensable men." Most of us know that our wives would say, ...that indispensable women are still alive.

So, if nobody is indispensable, why is the word used in the context of an indispensable person? The answer I believe is in the synonyms. When someone is thought to be indispensable, they are thought to be; essential, crucial, vital, imperative, absolutely necessary, needed, required, and requisite. Those words are powerful!

VALUES TO VALYOUABLE – A 3-STEP APPROACH TO RECOGNITION AND REWARDS

When you look at how you relate to a company or business, what words do you think of when it comes to yourself. What words do others use when they think of your role in the company?

Take a moment and think about those words, and write them in one column, and in the next, the words others would use for you. Most of us are more critical of our performance than others. We know in our hearts we could have done a little better, or we left something in the tank.

Mr. Kelley said, it is not about winning the meet, but how we performed individually. Did we get better? Did we beat our previous time? Many track records are thought to be unbreakable, but time and performance proves that a fallacy. So, the need is to have powerful words in our own column, but more importantly, in the column of our peers and management.

This list might help you to think of some related values –

Able	Education	Involved	Positive	Synergistic
Accountable	Effectiveness	Kind	Powerful	Teacher
Attitude	Emotion	Knowledge	Principled	Teamwork
Balance	Energetic	Leader	Proactive	Thoughtful
Behavior	Ethical	Learning	Quality	Thinker
Capability	Experience	Listening	Resourceful	Time manager
Character	Fair	Logical	Respectful	Trainer
Commitment	Flexible	Lover	Responsible	Trustworthy
Communication	Focus	Loyal	Responsive	Understanding
Conscience	Good	Manager	Result oriented	Valuable
Considerate	Guidance	Mature	Risk Taker	Visionary
Contribution	Habits	Motivation	Secure	Wise
Cooperation	Heart	Negotiator	Self-Aware	Worthy
Courage	Honest	Objective	Self-Manager	
Creativity	Imagination	Organizational	Sincere	
Delegation	Independent	Patient	Skilled	
Dependable	Influential	Perceptive	Strong	
Desire	Initiative	Performer	Structured	
Determination	Integrity	Personal	Supportive	
Doer	Interaction	Planner	Sympathetic	

VALUES TO VALYOUABLE – A 3-STEP APPROACH TO RECOGNITION AND REWARDS

Introduction to Values

There are several different aspects that would be wise to consider. Here's a list of some of the things that should be understood, so that values can be put into perspective. I want to use a simple description of these so that they can be differentiated in the future –

- Principles
- Values
- Ethics
- Behavior
- Goals
- Character

Principles are the rules and truths we live by and that should govern our actions. As our Declaration of Independence states; Life, Liberty and the Pursuit of Happiness. Covey explains them as; *"Principles are guidelines for human conduct that are proven to have enduring, permanent value. They're fundamental. They're essentially unarguable because they are self-evident."*

Some additional examples Covey uses are; *fairness, integrity, honesty, service, quality, excellence, potential, growth, patience, nurturance, and encouragement.*

Values are not to be confused with the value of something, such as monetary value or worth. Values in the context of this book are how we operate. They are not to be confused with goals, which get accomplished and get replaced with new ones. Values live on.

Covey talks about a *personal mission statement* or philosophy or creed. After he mentions our country's Constitution, I want to quote Covey; *"A personal mission statement based on correct principles becomes the same kind of standard for an individual. It becomes a personal constitution, the basis for making major, life-directing decisions, the basis for making daily decisions in the midst of the circumstances and emotions that affect our lives. It empowers individuals with the same timeless strength in the midst of change."*

Ethics is conforming to an accepted standard of good behavior, or the various principles listed above.

Behavior is how you act relative to principles. Consequences can be good or bad, depending on your actions.

An example would be how we obey speed limits. Most, if not all of us, exceed the limits. We are not alone and hope if someone is caught, it is the person going faster. We know what we are doing and know if we are the one caught there will be an adverse consequence. However, I would say in most cases, there is a tolerance observed by the police.

Goals are a target or an objective. They can be short or very long term, but they are something that drives actions and plans, and are meant to be accomplished.

Character is who we are, not who or what we say we are.

VALUES TO VALYOUABLE – A 3-STEP APPROACH TO RECOGNITION AND REWARDS

Impact of Values on Recognition and Rewards

My thoughts are that you are reading this book, and others, because you are not entirely satisfied with your personal results, and quite possibly, the recognition and rewards provided to date.

Once again, it is my thought that with defined, documented and followed personal values, your attitude will change and you will increase your focus, resulting in others, including management, noticing your actions and results. With better results comes recognition and rewards.

You need to judge the recognition and rewards you have received vs improvements after establishing and following your values:

With defined Values, your rewards could be so much greater -

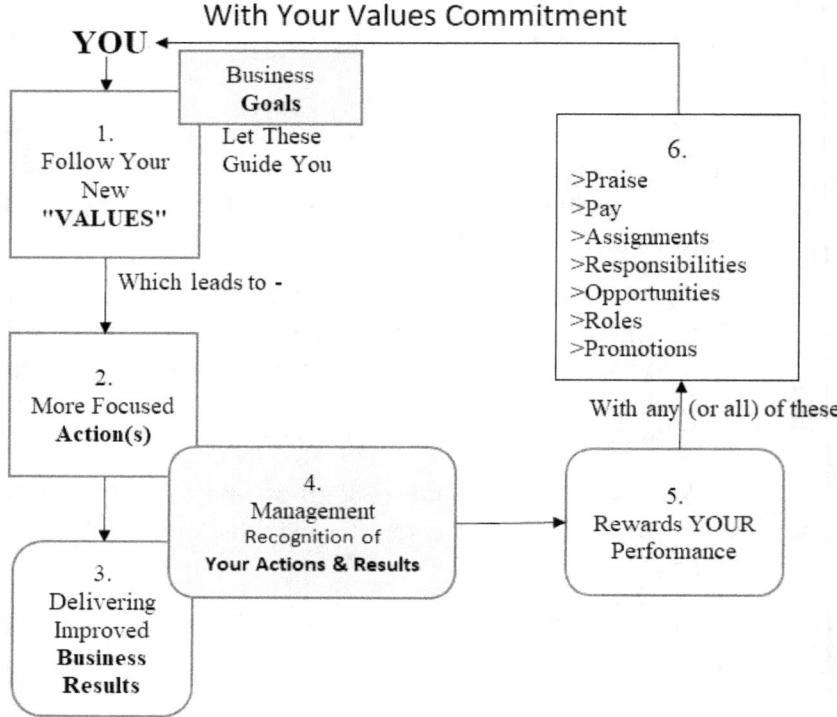

VALUES TO VALYOUABLE – A 3-STEP APPROACH TO RECOGNITION AND REWARDS

Values for Consideration
On a PERSONAL Level

❖ *Treat others as I would **CARE** to be treated.*

I think this is a great personal value to start my values list. How you treat others reflects almost everything you stand for. There are many examples of people who don't care about other people, or can't be bothered. One simple example is how much effort it takes to use directional signals. It makes sense, and in most cases, it is the law. However, many people just can't be bothered. How many times have you waited for a line of traffic to pass to allow you to enter the roadway, then some idiot makes a turn into the drive you are pulling out of? Totally inconsiderate.

I can honestly say I hold doors for everyone, use my directional signals, say please and thank you, recognize good service, and listen to others when they are talking. Why don't I bring this up to the technology of today – How many people talk on their phones when seated with others at a restaurant? Some even think that texting in the same situation is acceptable.

There is no excuse for not using good manners. I recommend this as one of your values. Others will indeed notice your behavior, and if it is a good one, they will have a good impression.

❖ *Always be **HONEST***

In the work environment this can indeed be a struggle. I have some stories related to this.

When you were the cause of a screw up, did you admit it? One thing I noticed having worked on the East coast versus the wild west. People in the east, seemed to immediately admit their mistake. Maybe I was lucky and worked with the right people. I think not. I believe it has something to do with being professional. They admit their mistake and work to resolve the impact. However, what I saw in the wild west was a new learning experience.

When the shit hit the fan and management asked how it happened, you would have thought there was a beautiful redhead walking by, as everyone looked around the room. It took new skills to analyze the situation to figure what went wrong and who might have been involved. Nobody is perfect and stuff happens. Please admit your mistakes and help everyone to learn from them.

Another story that taught me a lesson. We were in a joint meeting of the Information Systems group and the user community. There was a concern about whether the implementation date was known to be in jeopardy. When they looked at me for an answer, I told them we needed to reschedule. It was critically important because other things were going to happen in anticipation of the implementation. Well later, my boss called me to his office and read the riot act to me, and said I had stabbed him in the back. I was right to give them an honest answer, but I now understood who had the balls in the department.

The good news was that we implemented a work-around solution. It allowed the business to improve their operation, and delivered a much readier system solution later. The respect I gained by telling the truth to the user community allowed me to be a respected team member.

What I would offer you is to indeed be honest. The path of lies will get you to the wrong place.

- ❖ Build **CREDIBILITY** each and every day

This goes hand in hand with honesty. Trustworthiness is built on blocks of honesty; one weak block and the house comes crashing down. Credibility builds onto that by saying

VALUES TO VALYOUABLE – A 3-STEP APPROACH TO RECOGNITION AND REWARDS

what you mean, and doing what you say, or in others words being reliable. You can't fake results, and successful results are something everyone recognizes. My thoughts on this are how you act on a day-to-day basis. If you screw up, learn from it. The other values listed here will help immensely in this regard.

- ❖ Be a **VISIONARY** and provide **CREATIVE SOLUTIONS**

I could write a book on just this one value. The Readers Digest version is that I was given a gift. When I looked at business processes, I could see the problem areas, but more importantly, I could see how to do them much better. Many times, my thoughts and urgings were temporarily overlooked, especially when I was new to the organization. I had not earned my credibility yet.

However, there were two other capabilities I possessed. I would not go away. I would persist and try other forms of communication. I would draw flow diagrams and talk to the user community about my thoughts. Many times, they would say if my flow diagram of the way they did business was correct, no wonder they were having problems. Once I had the support of the business, it was easier to open eyes to better approaches.

The other thing I often did was to come up with a working model of the improved process. My job was more business analysis, but I knew how to write some code, and on one occasion when I couldn't get my idea across to management, I stayed nights and put together an application called "ATOM." It was an acronym for Analysis Toward Order Management. The problem I recognized was that when management had daily meetings to discuss the world-wide order status, there were considerable differences of opinion. I could sense the discrepancy was what order information was included. There were several buckets of data such as the type of holds, that could skew the numbers. My application took a copy of the world-wide order data and wrote a user-friendly program to ask and show in summary fashion what was included in that slice of order information.

When piloted by some of the key users, it became a daily application around the world. The key benefit is that management could agree on the numbers and deal with the issues instead of some of the smoke screens.

I'm not sure if everybody could include this value in their list, but it was one of mine and it gave me the personal license to go after other similar victories. Values are like puzzle pieces; they fit together to deliver improved results and better recognition.

- ❖ *LEARN from my mistakes*

Obviously, nobody is perfect. I have made some mistakes along the way. My biggest mistake was not fully focusing on becoming an architect. I started out in that direction, but life sent me in another.

The end result is that I wound up designing business/computer applications instead of buildings.

Today I have mixed emotions about college education. I believe young people are confused at their young age to know what they really want to do for the rest of their lives. They pursue a college education at much expense to themselves or their families. When they finish, they are one of the herd and competing for open positions.

Hopefully, you have completed this education process and already have a job. That is quite an accomplishment, and you should be proud of that.

VALUES TO VALYOUABLE – A 3-STEP APPROACH TO RECOGNITION AND REWARDS

In my day, it was much easier to get through the hiring process than it is today. It was more personal, and not as automated, which can throw your résumé out before it is even looked at by a person.

My hope is that this book will help you to identify the values that will lead you to more successful results and more recognition and rewards.

My thoughts are the best college graduates are the ones with actual related business experience. When I moved to Phoenix without a job, I had enough resources to live on, but what nobody picked me up on was my offer to work for a month for free. I knew after working at the company, they would want to hire me.

Once again, I'm getting off course here, but because I was coaching Little League, that network led to information about a job in town related to my experience with Wang Laboratories. I used my Values sheet for the first time to get that job.

My recommendation to you is that you will obviously make some mistakes. There is much to be learned from them. To ignore them is to have them repeated.

- ❖ Be a **CARING** person

I can honestly say that I never lost sleep at night because of how I treated another person. I had great bosses, who were helpful to my career. They were supportive and gave me enough room to use my strengths to deliver positive results. They indeed were key to my development and success.

On the flip side of this, I did work for a couple of bosses that I wondered how they slept at night, having treated people so badly.

I have coached many teams, and tried to do what Mr. Kelley did; assist their efforts with positive reinforcement. There is nothing that deflates a balloon as much as a pin of negative criticism. Everyone can do better. The words that someone gives, needs to build on the positives or the person will not feel good about themselves. Coaching a team is good experience as most team members have different skill levels.

One of my coaching experiences dealt with a tall boy who had never played baseball. He questioned many of the drills I conducted. One of them was why we were hitting golf whiffle balls. I told him if he could hit one of them, just think about what he would do to a baseball. He was a very memorable player. By the end of the season, not only was he a great hitter, but he was one of my best pitchers.

What is my point? If I had brushed him off instead of explaining things to him, he might have lost some interest in the game. I realized I needed to give him more attention than some of the other players, because he had not played before. Mr. Kelley was the best at believing that everyone could compete in track. He would try to recruit anyone and everyone. However, his caring approach allowed everyone to feel better about their individual efforts.

What I can offer to you is be as caring as you can be. You have no idea what the future holds in store for that person. Did my player wind up being a professional baseball player? I hope so.

Now that I covered some personal values and touched on coaching, let me talk about values related to management.

VALUES TO VALYOUABLE – A 3-STEP APPROACH TO RECOGNITION AND REWARDS

On a MANAGERIAL Level
❖ *LEAD BY EXAMPLE*

When I worked at Honeywell, there was a very effective vice-president who had a plaque over his door that read, "Lead, Follow or Get Out of the Way." He set an example in how he conducted himself, and lived by those words. I often think about his behavior and the results he obtained both at Honeywell and Wang Laboratories.

Someone once said it is better to ask for forgiveness than permission. If you know what you are trying to achieve, I believe it gives you the license to make decisions on your own.

I think I tried to set a favorable example, and just maybe, management recognized my performance. I made some mistakes along the way, but I was always working towards the best interest of the companies where I worked. There is a balance to keep in mind regarding what is required from a company standpoint and what is right for the customer.

I can remember the day I told my vice-president we were screwing up royally in one of our processes. He got tired of hearing me trying to improve customer results and asked me if I wanted to be the Director of Quality. What I did was right, and what we changed was right for the customer and our company.

❖ *My **SUCCESS** is the **SUM OF MY PEOPLES'** successes*

When President Kennedy was shot, I can remember exactly where I was standing when I heard the news. I can also remember where I was the day my manager asked me if I had considered being a project leader. I didn't answer him, but that night I had a restless night's sleep considering why I would want to jeopardize my success as an individual contributor versus relying on other people.

His encouragement the next day was the difference. He told me that everyone anguished about making a major change like that, but the things that drove me to success, would be the same things to impart on my people. He also said I was very detailed and that would be to my advantage being a project leader. His additional words were something like, "…just think of how much more results you could accomplish if you're not alone."

The rest is history. I later followed him from Honeywell to Wang Laboratories. We have stayed somewhat in touch, but I really need to reach out to him and buy him another lunch.

However, I have never lost touch with giving my different staff credit for what they have done. We collectively have done some amazing things. If you are ever presented with the same opportunity to manage people, I would recommend you go for it. Keep in mind as you accomplish things, just how much more you accomplish not being alone.

One other thing I would like to add is this – have you ever noticed how someone's eyes light up when you acknowledge their service. Try it someday. It gives me a warm feeling when I offer recognition for fine service. I'm sure it also benefits the person too.

VALUES TO VALYOUABLE – A 3-STEP APPROACH TO RECOGNITION AND REWARDS

❖ *Be **FAIR** and **CONSISTENT***

By now, I think you can tell I try to play by the rules. Another one of the life examples set by Mr. Kelley.

❖ *Point the right **DIRECTION** and strive for positive **RESULTS***

Having many people working for me, it was helpful to give them the right objective. More specifically, I tried to arm them with the power to make decisions themselves. Since we were going for total customer satisfaction, then make decisions that would give those results. If we made mistakes, and we were not always perfect, let the customer know that we will revise our processes to prevent it in the future, and offer the customer some compensation.

When customer calls were escalated to my office, we had already made one mistake. The fact they were asking for a higher level of recognition to help solve their problem, we were close to making a second mistake. Not handling customer problems effectively is a very weak branch to be sitting on. My belief is you do not get three strikes. By the time I was off the phone with most customers, they were telling me that my offers were not necessary. You can never do too much for any customer. If you were ever to lose one, it compounds into something much larger. The flip side is if you retain customers with good customer service, they are quick to recommend your services.

This is a good time to reference Mr. Kelley again. He offered suggestions for individual performance improvements and believed it is better to work for 'incremental improvements' instead of going for goals impossible to reach in one fell swoop.

I noticed he would recall every team member's last performance, and yell out when they were about to break their record. That was unbelievable support and an effective way of helping that person.

- ❖ *Be a good **EDUCATOR**, and share past successes and any failures*

This might be a good place to talk about my writing. When I first set out on this quest, I took an old novel I had drafted and revised it. I did an Internet search and found a publisher looking for promising new authors. I sent my manuscript, and to my surprise, they liked it and wanted to publish it. A few thousand dollars later I had a print copy of my novel. Great…not so fast.

What I later learned is that this publisher was a Vanity Press. For people unclear as to what that is, it is a way to get a book published, but it involves paying, not being paid. After learning about my mistake, I learned enough about the process to self-publish.

I now try to help other authors with the process to become self-published authors. I also caution them on the predators lurking just a few keystrokes away.

In my actual work career, I would put together training material and conduct training classes on new applications or system conversions. I'll talk about it later, but I included many pictures and screen shots which were a real help for anyone using the systems later.

When our company won the Arizona Association of Industries' *Manufacturer of the Year Award,* I shared with other companies my previously submitted documentation to help them with theirs. I also volunteered my services to the Association to help with their improvement initiatives.

VALUES TO VALYOUABLE – A 3-STEP APPROACH TO RECOGNITION AND REWARDS

❖ **CHALLENGE** *my team*

Maybe this comes from my coaching experience, but there is nothing like trying to inspire others to do their best. There was one story when I worked for Wang Laboratories.

The user community was questioning our Information Systems budget. I decided that we needed a visual to show the benefits to the business community for each of our projects. I challenged my team to provide the dollar savings for each open project, and the projects on the horizon.

When we were done, we had a large Apple tree drawing. Each apple had the estimated cost of the project and the planned savings. As we finished projects, we picked the apples and put them in a bushel basket. We communicated the accumulated savings. It helped to authorize our projects and to prioritize them. The business communities also used our figures to discuss prioritization with higher management.

❖ **HELP** *my people and others get where they want to go*

If one of these values can be ranked higher than some others, this one would rise near the top. It is often hard to help valuable members of my staff to get new higher-level positions. This is where I thanked them for their hard work. I would support their initiatives to seek those positions, and encourage them to go after positions where I thought they could do a good job.

I remember my manager asking me if I wanted to be a project leader. It changed my life, and I wanted to have the opportunity to pay it forward to others. One member left for an opportunity at Harvard, another wanted my encouragement for him to pursue starting his own marketing firm. In both cases I lost great employees, but who knows the impact they made at those firms.

Here's the biggest example of this value. I'm not writing this book for me, I'm writing it for you. I honestly believe what worked for me, will indeed work for you. I'm not sure what your values list will look like, but if it has some of mine, it is sure to have other people notice you more than they do today. If you have read this book this far, I acknowledge your desire to help yourself. You are on the right track.

If you need to talk to me personally about something I can help with, my contact information will be included at the back of the book. Please contact me, and I'll try my best to help.

To know whether this book is indeed helping readers, reviews and testimonials are always appreciated. If this book does help someone, your input might just help someone else.

- ❖ **DELEGATE** *responsibility, but maintain focus on results*

I mentioned this somewhat in the pointing the right direction and striving for results. I gave my quality staff the authorization to do what they needed to do when we failed to provide quality results. This was giving them the license not to ask for permission, but to do what they felt was required in the situation. One person can't do it all, and if you point the right direction and give them the license, they will do their best to get the correct results.

- ❖ **REWARD** *the performance that I need repeated*

VALUES TO VALYOUABLE – A 3-STEP APPROACH TO RECOGNITION AND REWARDS

One compliment is more powerful than ten discussions about shortcomings. I recommend you look for every opportunity to give even daily feedback to staff members about their efforts you want them, and others, to repeat. Many times, there are programs such as Employee of the Month that are helpful, but everyone recommended should be rewarded, not just the winner.

I also have mixed emotions about the annual review processes. Many times, at different companies, there are controls about amounts that can be given. The worst of these is the cap placed on each area. If you were the owner of the company, would you want any employee not to be adequately rewarded for their efforts? I think not, but many times after awarding good employees with their increases, it was not fair. One way to think of this is if a group had all great results and obviously great employees, why give those people a forced balanced total percentage?

I know I will take some criticism for the above, but if it was my company, I would give them increases that recognize their individual contributions rather than a forced or leveled increase. I think the future might support changes in this area. I hope so.

- ❖ **HIRE** *the people with the* **RIGHT** *personal ATTRIBUTES*

Here is another area where I believe my values are in contrast with the accepted methods. Companies will look for candidates who have great credentials such as educations from highly recognized institutions, significant training, skills, experiences, capabilities etc. I think the person who possesses the right personal attributes like these listed here in these values, will deliver equal if not better results to a company.

Attitude is one of the attributes that can be witnessed in an interview. However, if the candidate is overlooked for the interview, what has that company lost in positive results? I know I am looking at this from the underdog position, but I know the results I provided to the companies I worked for. I earned my pay, and more than returned it with many great improvements.

Another story. I hired a young man who came across in a very positive way. When I recommended hiring him, I think it was Human Resources that learned about his earlier felony. I followed up with the candidate and asked specifically about the circumstances. He convinced me that he was no longer that person and had paid his price. After the battle to hire him, he surpassed my expectations and was very gifted at representing business flow diagrams, which was what we needed. He was a great hire. From time to time, he manages to find me and to say hello. I hope I helped him to get where he needed to go.

You can state values, but when you live by them, they really do mean something.

- ❖ *Strive to be the **BEST**, or one of the best managers*

Once again, I think back on the transition from an individual contributor to a project leader. If I had not taken that opportunity, who knows where I would have wound up. More importantly, what would have not been delivered by my various staffs? I'm sure I wasn't the best manager, but I did try to be one of the best. I will leave it up to my managers and those staffs to comment.

I do believe my increased responsibilities including reaching four different director-level positions tells an interesting story. In case you are wondering; they were with MicroAge QIS in Tempe Arizona, and the positions were;

VALUES TO VALYOUABLE – A 3-STEP APPROACH TO RECOGNITION AND REWARDS

Director of Quality, Director of Operations, Director of Quality and Project Management, and Director of New Business Development.

MicroAge Quality Integration Services (QIS) is the company that won the Arizona Association of Industries' *Manufacturer of the Year Award* two years in a row.

I want to thank all my managers for their support and guidance.

On a BUSINESS Level
❖ *Make **DECISIONS** as though the company were my own*

I recommend this as one of your own values. There are many times when decisions need to be made very quickly, and having this value as a guide will indeed come in handy.

A story – I had just been hired by MicroAge. Ralph, the vice president who hired me, and I flew to Ohio to introduce me to our branch manager there and to discuss the project I was being assigned. That local branch was doing a network server install over the upcoming weekend and needed the equipment on site to do some installation prep work. The insurance company needed to be up and running the following Monday morning. My role was to see that the configuration of the equipment was done to specification and delivered according to schedule. What will go wrong will go wrong, and it will go wrong at the worst possible time.

I think it was a Wednesday, but it was my second week. Several things happened.

The first was that the configuration of computer equipment due to ship that day was not ready. Not familiar with the process, I asked the manager of the configuration department what the problem was. He indicated that the configuration would be completed the next day, but would definitely not make the cutoff for UPS shipments that day, and the technician would be leaving. I told him I wanted the configuration completed, and if the tech couldn't complete the configuration, he needed to find someone to finish it as soon as possible. I communicated with Ralph to let him know the status and what I was planning to do. I could tell by his side of the conversation that he was letting me run with this.

VALUES TO VALYOUABLE – A 3-STEP APPROACH TO RECOGNITION AND REWARDS

After letting the manager know I had communicated with Ralph, and some, let me call it negotiation, he consented to have the tech stay and finish the work. He kind of smiled when I told him I would worry about making the arrangements to get the order shipped. Not knowing any of the people necessary to pull this off, I did manage to get the help in the shipping department to get it picked up and placed on the same flight as mine going out the next morning.

My next problem was how to get it picked up at the airport and delivered to the installation site. Once again, I was not familiar with who to call, but with help, we did arrange for a company to pick up the equipment and get it delivered.

My next problem came when I was at the airport trying to get a rental car. They would not take cash and I did not have a credit card. That is another whole story and not going to be covered here. I tracked down the driver who was picking up the equipment and requested that I ride with him to the delivery site.

So, this was my first experience at that company trying to do what I needed to do to meet the planned weekend installation. The branch manager was at the insurance company installation site and was surprised to see me arriving with the delivery.

My next call was to Ralph to update him that we were on schedule and to alert him I was planning to stay over the weekend to participate in the installation.

The installation was a success and I took some notes and pictures and later provided an installation report to Ralph. He embarrassed me by showing it to the project manager lead, indicating that we had just raised the bar for our project management group.

The interesting thing and the lesson here - all of those people and groups, including shipping, wound up working for me. I made those early decisions as though the company were mine, and realized later that my focus on making project deadlines was a key factor in subsequent promotions.

❖ Be a good *BUSINESS PARTNER*

The story above ties in with this value. All my project assignments during my early years with MicroAge involved making sure that our configuration center met our end of project deadlines.

One of my favorite assignments was being the project manager for our configuration center in support of our Orange County branch. There were many different projects and after working remotely, and on site, with the branch associates, I considered many of them friends. I'm also sure when it came time for me to accept additional responsibilities, Robin, the branch manager was very supportive. None of my additional management responsibilities would have happened if Lou had not encouraged me to accept a leadership role, and I honestly believe my values sheet played an important role as well. Once again, I would like to thank my managers for their support.

❖ *KNOW the business*

One of my strengths is that I am very detailed. There is a funny story I will relate to that after this introduction.

Maybe the weakness I have is that I need to picture the business processes. Without adequate process documentation to review, I would have to walk the processes

VALUES TO VALYOUABLE – A 3-STEP APPROACH TO RECOGNITION AND REWARDS

myself. If I did not actually draw the processes, step by step, my mind did capture the flow. However, it was how my mind worked, and I would say nine times out of ten I would make process flow diagrams. Not only did that help me, but it helped the business and our systems people.

When I worked in the materials area of Honeywell, I would often have documentation of our business processes. Jim, the director in the systems area, noticed my documentation and offered me a position in the systems group. That was one of the doors that changed my career. From that time on, I had a career in the information systems area. Jim felt that my ability to understand and document process flows could help the systems department better define applications for the other business areas. Once again thanks to one of my managers.

Here's what I consider a funny story. After MicroAge filed for bankruptcy and I had a few years running my own company, I felt I needed better health insurance. The company I wanted to work for was Sun Health. After making several attempts at filling out their employment application paperwork, I had an offer at another company. I called the Human Resources department and asked why I had not received any interviews, and told them about the latest position for which I had applied. I also mentioned I had an offer at another company and wanted to work for Sun Health.

About two hours later, I received a call from Patrick, the manager who had the open position. He told me he didn't know where any of my paperwork went, but he would like to provide me with an interview. It was already near the end of the day, but I asked if we could do it that afternoon. He consented to give me an interview the following morning.

During the interview with Patrick and one of the department leads, Emma asked me why I would want to work for what they could offer, since I was making tens of thousands more when I worked for MicroAge. She later told me she was worried I would take the position and leave at the first opportunity of something more in line with my former pay.

I said that if they hired me, I would not leave the company, it would be my last job, as I was close to retirement age. I also told them I needed health insurance more than I needed a large pay check.

Unknown to me at that time, I developed two cancers, and after two surgeries, I decided the stress of my dad's failing health, surgeries, and pressures at work, it was time to retire. I gave them five years.

Oh yeah, the funny story! In my original interview,. Patrick asked me what anyone had said negative about me, and I answered, I was very detailed. When things would require a discussion about what went wrong, we would laugh when I echoed the words that I was very detailed. We both thought it was funny even to this day, but you probably don't see it as that. I should also say that Patrick and I are close friends. I often mention to him that if he hadn't believed in me, and hired me, that I'm not sure what the consequences would have been of not having good health insurance.

When I was saying my goodbyes to the different areas I worked for, the other lead, who was normally very private, gave me a hug and mentioned her earlier concern about leaving and that I had kept my word. She also told me that I was a good hire and she had learned many things from me, and thanked me. Her sharing her thoughts touched my heart, and I know she could tell. Once again, I had to thank someone who had a positive effect on my life.

VALUES TO VALYOUABLE – A 3-STEP APPROACH TO RECOGNITION AND REWARDS

❖ *Don't present problems without*
   SUGGESTIONS/SOLUTIONS

How many times have you been in a meeting and there is a discussion about problems? How many times do you hear those same people offer suggestions?

I can think of ways we could change how to make our legislature more effective, but I'm sure it would be another case of we can't do that. I also try to avoid discussions of politics. However, a simple analogy is we don't run companies or even sports teams the way we run our country. Enough said.

My thoughts are that if you discover a problem, look for what has changed. One of the great training courses I took was Kepner-Tregoe, which provided a systematic method to identify the root cause of problems.

I strongly suggest that you consider this value in your own. There are many problems that can and will surface when companies are changing their business and operations. Management would surely recognize employees who can offer some suggestions/solutions, or appreciate offers to investigate. Remember, if it was your company, what would you want to see or hear?

When the problem came up with different order management data, attempts at making suggestions to resolve the problem came with skepticism because with any application or system, it involved resources and significant time. I believed I had the right solution and was willing to invest my own time to deliver a working solution. I earned Wang's highest award for that effort. However, I wasn't looking for the award, I was trying to resolve the problem.

With each passing day we were missing taking the right steps to manage our world-wide order backlog.

There is another value that ties in with this one – go after victories that are worth winning. Sometimes it just takes believing in a solution enough to commit your butt. I'm reminded of that vice-president's sign – 'Lead, Follow, or get out of the way!'

VALUES TO VALYOUABLE – A 3-STEP APPROACH TO RECOGNITION AND REWARDS

On a PROJECT Level

❖ *Keep it **SIMPLE**, and **ADD COMPLEXITY** over time*

I realized somewhere along my career that if I tried to convey all the information I had, it would confuse my audience. So, I developed a strategy where I would do a simple process flow of the major steps. When there was some interest in the flow, I would then add more detail to help explain how things interacted. This tied in closely with building a working model of the process, or the application.

One of the projects we had at MicroAge was to supply computer products daily to Kodak in Rochester NY. They had established methods that our New York Branch indicated we had to use. However, the volume of orders and items quickly surpassed our existing methods to comply efficiently and effectively. Every item they ordered needed an individual corresponding item slip for the Kodak receiver to recognize and receive in their system. Many times, there wasn't enough room on the box to place all of these slips. With the help of a programming person from the outside, he was able to take my concept which combined our existing process steps with the result required by Kodak.

We were eventually able to convince them of an even more efficient process that met their receiver process, and allowed us to reduce data discrepancies. We even teamed up with UPS to eliminate their handling of individual boxes, replacing it with a single consolidated "Igloo" shipment from our facility right into the UPS aircraft. We could give Kodak a daily data file of the contents that they could mass receive. This reduced the number of data discrepancies and improved cash flow.

Trying to jump to the top most step would have not only confused everybody, but it would not have been successful. I can't say enough about Jim and our branch team in New York, who brokered discussions with their very important client. The systems management at Kodak was also instrumental in getting the accounting departments to accept the more efficient and accurate process.

- ❖ *Start with a **SOLID FOUNDATION** and go from there*

At this point I would like to say that my values fit together and get strength from each other. When I started this book, my thoughts were that each person could identify their own values, but I think there is some potential benefit to consider my list as it is integrated and might significantly help your performance.

Another story – Dennis, who was the vice-president at Wang Laboratories who hired me, met me at a social function. I told him what I did at Honeywell, and he casually said if I had any thoughts of considering Wang, I should contact him. Many of our employees at Honeywell were making a transition to Wang, including one of my former managers.

I was new to the company, and many learned Dennis had backed my being hired. That might not have been in my favor. However, my role was that of a systems consultant. One of the first things I was thrown into was a multi-million-dollar bottleneck within the warehouse.

Orders were being allocated from the main warehouse, but because of individual shortages, they sat in the staging area waiting for the missing product. Upon investigation, I became aware that some of the missing items were sitting on other orders, which were waiting on other material.

VALUES TO VALYOUABLE – A 3-STEP APPROACH TO RECOGNITION AND REWARDS

My concept of what was happening was like a super market with people trying to fill their shopping lists, but couldn't because other people had some of the 'short supply' items in their carts. When I discussed this with the management responsible, I used that analogy, and said we needed to review each person's shopping list (i.e., the orders) before we released them for picking. If they weren't complete, we should review the next priority order. The result was that orders wouldn't be released for picking unless they could be filled completely. Once picked they could be shipped without any delay.

We wound up building, very quickly, a manual system of prescreened orders before releasing them for picking. A list of any order shortages was also captured and used to expedite product manufacture or procurement. The systems group built an application between the two existing order and warehouse production systems. The new application was titled "Supermarket."

- ❖ Build a **WORKING MODEL**, of what the user needs/solution is

As you might remember, I had some whip marks from my boss when I said we needed to reschedule our planned installation.

With the help of a very efficient Basic programmer, we built a working model of the delayed production system. We took this workaround solution to one of our factories and piloted the production system process using the temporary system. At one point, it was thought that the workaround system might suffice to be the production system. However, there was too much manual effort to handle just one facilities data from the production system.

We did use the temporary application to build some of the user system documentation which helped with system training and eventual implementation. Without the help of Doug, the systems manager at that facility, we would not have been successful with this pilot. There could have been some politics involved in this temporary implementation, but what everyone observed was a close-knit team working together for the success of the company. Thanks Doug!

- ❖ **OBTAIN THE INPUT(S)** *of knowledgeable users*

What I have observed is that there are many people within the business community, who, for one reason or another, are very familiar with the way things are done. When you encourage them to share their knowledge, the information they provide is priceless.

I could look at existing processes and come up with business process flows. However, in many cases, there are subtle nuances involved, which if not correctly highlighted, might impact the way applications are designed and built.

Before we designed and built the very large order processing system at Honeywell, which I talked about before, we had a series of user walkthrough sessions that walked the order processes step by step. Without the user participation, and management support for their time, our systems group would have missed important details.

I forgot this lesson when I wrote my first novel. Shame on me. I should have touched base with others who had published novels before. I could have saved several thousand dollars, and avoided delays in getting my story published.

Now, I'm trying to be one of the knowledgeable users for other authors who want to become published authors.

VALUES TO VALYOUABLE – A 3-STEP APPROACH TO RECOGNITION AND REWARDS

- ❖ *Run a **NO SURPRISES** operation*

Communication is a key word here. There was a time when I was the EDP systems manager at Honeywell when my boss kept asking about project status. Being a picture-oriented person, I took the smaller blank IBM punch cards and used each one to write a description of each project, specifically the name and some of the project details.

On my wall, I put each card under the functional project area. On one side were the active projects, and the projects in queue; and on the other side were the completed projects. What I learned quickly is that my boss could come in at any time, and see what projects were completed previously, as well as newly completed, and where the other projects stood. I also used the newly completed projects to do part of my monthly report.

One of my former managers took a picture of my wall with all the projects, framed it and presented it to me at my going away party.

When I was burning the night oil working on the ATOM application, my boss eventually noticed my late hours, and asked what the hell I was doing. Once again, I was not asking for permission, I was most certainly not doing my primary responsibility. I was writing Basic code. By the time he learned what I was doing, it was not in anyone's interest to stop me.

One of my other stated values "Go after victories that are worth winning."

Of a GENERAL Nature
❖ ***DON'T FIX** something that isn't broken*

There are many things that truly need to be addressed in major corporations. Trying to make processes more efficient and effective can have significant bottom line benefits, but trying to fix something that isn't broken, is a major waste of time.

In the information systems area, we always had a backlog of projects which needed to be prioritized and worked on.

This is almost a common-sense value, but having it listed prevents falling into a trap. The caution here is that you can break what is working.

❖ *Go after **VICTORIES** that are worth winning*

Many times, we are unfortunately presented with a potential course of action that is oppositional to popular opinion. There is a major risk to going after these major challenges. A person's credibility can be at stake, should that course be followed, and wind up a disaster.

The balance that needs to be evaluated is whether that course of action is in the best interest of the department, branch, or company. Is it truly worth winning?

In my career, I have been lucky in this regard. I can't say I made decisions easily when it came to things in this area, but when I did, I had a good idea that it was the right choice to make. I think the expression to consider here is – Is it better to have tried and failed, than to have never tried?

Let me give you a couple of examples, which I mentioned earlier. Going after the Manufacturer of the Year award was a considerable undertaking. It involved filling out a very detailed application package. When I talked to my boss and

VALUES TO VALYOUABLE – A 3-STEP APPROACH TO RECOGNITION AND REWARDS

my peers about going for this award, they said it was probably a waste of time. Despite their views, I knew how good our organization was. We were also ISO9001, which meant we had pretty much a zero-defects organization.

I decided that it was right to go after the recognition. I was not out on this branch alone, as other staff members had to provide some of the detail needed in the application package, but it was clear who owned it.

The short story is we did win the award. However, at the announcement ceremony, the three companies on the short list were present at the dinner meeting. My boss and his boss were there. It would have been embarrassing for me if we lost, but what was done was done. When we won, I felt an immediate relief. There was much celebration within the organization later, and once again, I had built more credibility. However, all I did was take on the responsibility for the application process, it was the organization that fully deserved the recognition.

I had the same kind of resistance the next year when I recommended, we go for the award again. I didn't learn my lesson, or maybe I did. I recommended we try to receive Industry Weeks recognition as one of the top manufacturing companies. In both cases, we indeed succeeded.

I think you will know when significant opportunities are presented to you, but I encourage you to have this value as one of yours. The main point of this book is to have values that will change your attitude and actions to ultimately receive better recognition and rewards. Major challenges offer major potential for good things to happen to you. Go for them!

❖ *Be a **SIGNIFICANT TEAM PLAYER***

I was not always the best player on a team. However, a team obviously includes other members, and collectively, a team is more capable than any of its parts. A person can only do his/her best.

Working in a department or a company is like a sports team. There are things that need to be done, roles that need to be performed, and most importantly, goals that need to be accomplished.

This value is one of the values I did decide to rework. Originally, I had this as Replace Politics with Teamwork. However, and unfortunately, politics exists in a company, and I didn't want to have people missing out on the overall intent of my values.

However, I strongly believe that politics within a company is costly. I observed at one of the companies I worked for, vice-presidents and directors doing everything they could to have the newly appointed leader fail. They wound up shooting themselves in the foot, because as the person failed, so did the company. The company declared bankruptcy and the company stock (and theirs) became worthless. This was politics at its worst, because it impacted so many other innocent people. It was also the catalyst that forced me to move to Arizona.

Back to the team analogy. They not only lost the game, they lost the season, and their ability to play. Hopefully, it was a lesson well learned.

Another similar situation that resulted in bankruptcy was at another company. They split the company into two distinct parts, which resulted in an internal competition. My analogy of this is to take money from one pocket and put it in the other. Since they were charging each other for their services. The bottom line is that you don't go to the bank with any

VALUES TO VALYOUABLE – A 3-STEP APPROACH TO RECOGNITION AND REWARDS

new funds. In essence, the company created two competing teams.

❖ **COMMUNICATE WELL**, or *don't add to the confusion*

Normally, I am a quiet, sit and listen, type of person. When I hear discussions, I often mentally put the details into a picture. When I finally can't stand it any longer, I will get up and draw a picture on the white board, or on a flip chart. What I found is that it helps clarify the different viewpoints and expedites direction.

Using this method, I am not adding another viewpoint, but only helping everyone to get on the same page.

❖ **ANTICIPATE** and **PLAN** *accordingly*

Good project managers think of what can go wrong, and plan for it. We all know things happen, and having planned actions avoids delays. As mentioned earlier, building a working model and doing a pilot implementation can help flesh out the process. Just doing a step-by-step guideline can help with identifying the potential roadblocks.

One of the lessons learned about project failure is a change of scope. If someone asks for even a slight change in direction, I caution you to carefully consider the potential risks. When I worked for Honeywell, we used outside software development firms to develop the software for us. That organization had learned the dangers of scope change, and had every one of our requested changes go through a formal change in scope request, review, and authorization process.

❖ *Communicate with **"PICTURES"** to facilitate common understanding*

I guess my wanting to be an architect played an important role in my drawing pictures, flow diagrams and other documentation. I often said that instead of designing buildings, I was designing applications and systems.

Regardless, if you can capture anything in a picture, you will enable many different existing mental images to focus on a common understanding. A picture is worth a thousand words. People have their own ways of assimilating things; it is best to drive to a common view.

When our dinner group was having the men do the cooking for our next gathering, I had a problem understanding the recipe I was given. After much frustration, I finally did a flow diagram of that recipe. Not only did that dish turn out correctly, the women learned about my flow diagram. When they looked it over, they said I should write a cook book. I think someone must have done that by now.

❖ *Provide an **"ANYTHING CAN BE DONE"** attitude with results*

I have a strong belief that if your mind can visualize something, it can be something that can be done. To test what I mean by this - if you think people can't get younger, it's because you've been programmed not to think outside the box. I think that although we can't understand how this is possible today, at some time, we will find a method to do exactly that. Another example is - you can't bring someone back alive. I challenge you to look at the number of people who have opted for Cryogenics (i.e., being frozen), waiting

VALUES TO VALYOUABLE – A 3-STEP APPROACH TO RECOGNITION AND REWARDS

for a cure for their disease. They believed that anything can be done.

We are obviously spending considerable amounts of money trying to find a cure for many cancers. There will come a day when cancer will be like other eradicated diseases.

YOU need to believe that by reading this book and identifying your values, listing them, and following them, that you will change your outlook and attitude and do some things you wouldn't have ever considered before. Management can't afford not to notice your actions and your results. Even if you fail, they will give you credit for trying. Their recognition will result in more rewards for you.

Summary List of My Values
On a PERSONAL Level –

- Treat others as I would **CARE** to be treated
- Always be **HONEST**
- Build **CREDIBILITY** each and every day
- Be a **VISIONARY** and provide **CREATIVE SOLUTIONS**
- **LEARN** from any mistakes
- Be a **CARING** person

On a MANAGERIAL Level –

- **LEAD BY EXAMPLE**
- My **SUCCESS** is the **SUM OF MY PEOPLES'** successes
- Be **FAIR** and **CONSISTENT**
- Point the right **DIRECTION** and strive for positive **RESULTS**
- Be a good **EDUCATOR**, and share past successes and any failures
- **CHALLENGE** my team
- **HELP** my people and others get where they want to go
- **DELEGATE** responsibility, but maintain focus on results
- **REWARD** the performance that I need repeated
- **HIRE** the people with the **RIGHT ATTRIBUTES**
- Strive to be the **BEST**, or one of the best managers

VALUES TO VALYOUABLE – A 3-STEP APPROACH TO RECOGNITION AND REWARDS

On a BUSINESS Level –

- Make **DECISIONS** as though the company was my own
- Be a good **BUSINESS PARTNER**
- **KNOW** the business
- Don't present problems without **SUGGESTIONS/SOLUTIONS**

On a PROJECT Level –

- Keep it **SIMPLE** and **ADD COMPLEXITY** over time
- Start with a **SOLID FOUNDATION** and go from there
- Build a **WORKING MODEL** of what the user needs/solution is
- **OBTAIN THE INPUT**(s) of knowledgeable users
- Run a **NO SURPRISES** operation

Of a GENERAL Level –

- Don't fix something that isn't broken
- Go after **VICTORIES** that are worth winning
- Be a **SIGNIFICANT TEAM PLAYER**
- **COMMUNICATE WELL**, or don't add to the confusion
- **ANTICIPATE** and **PLAN** accordingly
- Communicate with **"PICTURES"** to facilitate common understanding
- Provide an **"ANYTHING CAN BE DONE"** attitude with results

My Credentials

I have years of education, but never completed my degree. In my opinion, that adds credibility to the approach covered in this book. If the approach worked for me, what potential is there for you?

If you recall, I mentioned there were times when I believed in something so much that I went for it, despite what others thought about the direction. This book is exactly that case – I believe it will indeed help many people.

I truly hope that it can help you. Once again, if it does, I would like to hear your success story. Those stories will help prove my point.

Once again, I am repeating myself –

What I do have that I'm proud of, and why I'm writing this book for you, is positive personal results based on a simple set of values, which you can construct in as little as a day for yourself.

I have over forty years working for various Fortune 500 companies. My background includes working my way up from the ground floor in a mailroom, to holding several director-level positions. I obtained my real estate broker's license, but never really focused on that career.

Working in Information Systems, I became a PMI certified project management professional (PMP). I value my creativity and analytical capabilities. Many times, my ability to see a better way of doing things has led to improved company results. I am currently a self-published author of eight books, including a five book mystery series.

VALUES TO VALYOUABLE – A 3-STEP APPROACH TO RECOGNITION AND REWARDS

I am now retired and don't need to write this book for me. However, once again, one of my personal values is to

> ***HELP*** *my people, and others, get where they want to go.*

I'm writing this book for you. I cannot guarantee success or changes to your career, but I sincerely hope this effort is not a waste of my time and yours. I would like to think this book is my legacy, rather than the positive results I left at the companies where I worked.

I've done some amazing things, many of which I doubted could be done, but I was driven to deliver because of a simple personal mission statement (values). I believe there are many more positive results to be had if I encourage YOU to give this simple method a try. If it helps even one of you, who knows the benefit it will have?

Closing Remarks

Mr. Kelley's passing is a reminder that life is short. We all want to be remembered for what we made better while we were here. He lived his life for the family of students and athletes he encountered. Many lives, if not all, were changed in such a special way by this man. He never truly understood the impact he had on so many people. In my opinion, he gave us the will to never give up and to constantly try to do our best to improve.

I look around at the awards I still display and the thing I am proudest of is not there. The award cannot be seen by anyone. It is in my heart. It is the knowledge that I did my best to earn my pay, and to know that others respect what I did for them and their company.

I write fiction novels for my own enjoyment. However, I feel compelled to write this book to potentially help others to have this same knowledge and respect. I am trying my part to carry Mr. Kelley's stick. I wish I could hear him saying his words of encouragement, but I don't need to hear them, they are in my heart. With much love, thank you Mr. Kelley!

Remember this – businesses will find it hard to dispense with a person who they feel is indispensable, or neglect paying them.

This book has been about my values and experiences. Mr. Kelley inspired me years ago and most recently. However, my workplace career is over, but my sincere hope is that this book will inspire YOU to identify your Compass of Values and enable you to drive the bus. May you have much success, recognition and many rewards.

Thank you for purchasing this book and for taking the time to read it.

If this book manages to add to even one reader's behavior and success, it will have been worth this effort. Success stories are always welcome!

DickCWaters@gmail.com

Index

abilities, 28
admit, 39, 40
annual review, 51
Arizona Association of Industries, 22, 48
ATOM, 41, 65
attitude, 19, 37, 70
Attitude, 52
Basic code, 65
behavior, 26, 36, 39, 45, 77
Behavior, 35, 36
belief, 27, 47
believed in me, 58
best, 19, 21, 22, 43, 44, 45, 49, 50, 52, 76
better results, 37
caring approach, 44
cash flow, 61
Character, 35, 36
characteristics, 26
coached, 43
Communication, 65
compass, 22, 23
Compass of Values, 21, 31, 76
consequence, 36
Covey, 23, 24, 35, 36
credentials, 51, 74
customer satisfaction, 21, 47
daily feedback, 51
data discrepancies, 61

desire, 50
detailed, 46, 56, 58
directional signals, 39
Director, 45, 53
dispense, 32, 76
document, 23, 26, 27, 57
drive the bus, 24, 26, 76
education, 42
Education, 18
Employee of the Month, 51
encouragement, 35, 46, 50, 76
Ethics, 35, 36
example, 22, 36, 39, 45, 50
experience, 40, 43, 44, 49
Experience, 18
flow diagrams, 41, 52, 57
follow, 26
Fortune 500, 74
goal, 42
goals, 24, 31, 35, 47
Goals, 24, 35
Golden rule, 25
guide, 31, 54
Habit, 23
Harvard, 49
Honeywell, 45, 46, 57, 62, 64, 65
HOW, 19, 24
Igloo, 61
impact, 27, 40, 50, 64, 76

VALUES TO VALYOUABLE – A 3-STEP APPROACH TO RECOGNITION AND REWARDS

inconsiderate, 39
incremental improvements, 47
indispensable, 32, 76
individual contributor, 46, 52
Industry Week Magazine, 22
inspire, 49, 76
inspire others, 49
interview, 21, 23, 26, 52, 57, 58
Kelley, 29, 76
Kepner-Tregoe, 59
know yourself, 18
Knowledge, 18
Kodak, 61, 62
Learning, 18
license, 26, 27, 42, 45, 50, 74
life, 21, 23, 28, 31, 36, 47, 49, 58, 76
life-changing, 23
live by them, 52
manners, 39
Manufacturer of the Year, 22, 48
manuscript, 48
motivation, 27, 29
Mr. Kelley, 27, 28, 29, 33, 43, 44, 47, 76
neglect, 32, 76
network, 43, 54
never give up, 27, 76
New York Branch, 61
Noing you, 18
Not Getting, 18
not giving up, 19
One compliment, 51
opportunities, 21
Orange County, 56
path of lies, 40
pay it forward, 29, 49
performance, 22, 27, 28, 31, 33, 45, 47, 50, 62
personal mission statement, 23, 24, 36, 75
Personal Mission Statement, 19, 31
personal satisfaction, 27
phones, 39
pin of negative criticism, 44
PMI, 74
positive habits, 18
positive impact, 28
positive reinforcement, 43
positive results, 18, 19, 43, 52, 75
possess, 18, 19, 26
power to make decisions, 47
powerful, 32, 33, 51
President Kennedy, 45
principles, 36
Principles, 35
process flow, 57, 61
professional, 40, 44, 74

programmed, 30
promotions, 21, 56
publisher, 48
puzzle pieces, 42
quality, 21, 35, 50
recognition, 18, 22, 27, 37, 42, 46, 47
recognize, 31, 39, 51, 59, 61
recognized, 19, 23, 26, 27, 29, 41, 45, 51
respect, 40, 76
results, 19, 21, 37, 41, 42, 43, 45, 46, 47, 48, 50, 51, 52, 70, 74, 75
reviews, 50
rewarded, 19, 29, 51
rewards, 18, 37
self-publish, 48
service, 24, 29, 35, 39, 43, 46, 47
set an example, 45
skills, 40, 51
Skills, 18
stand for, 25, 31, 39
stick, 28, 29, 76
strategy, 61
success, 43, 46, 55, 64, 75, 76, 77
successful, 24, 26, 29, 41, 62, 64

Sun Health, 57
Supermarket, 63
support, 24, 31, 41, 49, 51, 53, 56, 64
team, 24, 27, 28, 31, 40, 44, 49, 62, 64
testimonials, 50
texting, 39
Three simple steps, 18
tick, 19, 23, 31
training, 42, 48, 51, 59, 64
Training, 18
training material, 48
truth, 40
UPS, 54, 61
valuable, 27, 49
values, 18, 19, 22, 23, 24, 25, 26, 27, 30, 31, 35, 37, 39, 41, 44, 49, 50, 51, 52, 74, 75
values fit together, 62
Vanity Press, 48
Wang, 21, 43, 45, 46, 49, 59, 62
workaround solution, 63
working model, 41, 61, 63
writing, 24, 48, 50, 65, 74, 75

Bibliography

Covey, Stephen R. *The 7 Habits of Highly Effective People,* (NY: Simon & Schuster, 1989, *25th Anniversary Edition* 2013),

"Principles" Defined with Examples

    Pg. 42-43

"Seven Habits" Listed and Defined

    Pg. 59-60

A Personal Mission Statement... Philosophy or Creed

    Pg *113*

A Personal Mission Statement... Personal Constitution

    Pg *115*

Author Books and Amazon Page
Dick C. Waters

Introduction to Novels and Anthologies

Scott Tucker Serial-Killer Mystery Series -

Branded for Murder
Serial Separation
Scent of Gardenia
Fragrance of Revenge
Foreplay for Murder

Romance Novel – (Dixie Waters)
You Complete My Heart

Anthologies -
2013 Flash Fiction Anthology
Heart to Heart Anthology

Link to Amazon Author Page -

https://www.amazon.com/Dick-Waters/e/B007K8J222

(Includes Many Book-Trailer Videos)

www.ingramcontent.com/pod-product-compliance
Lightning Source LLC
Chambersburg PA
CBHW050251220526
45465CB00002B/638